50 NIFTY SUPER Friendship Crafts

Written by Sharon McCoy
Additional material by Joanna Siebert

Illustrated by Charlene Olexiewicz

LOWELL HOUSE JUVENILE

LOS ANGELES

CONTEMPORARY BOOKS

CHICAGO

NOTE: The numbered bracelet above the heading of each craft indicates the level of difficulty, 1 being the easiest, 3 being the hardest.

Publisher: Jack Artenstein
Director of Publishing Services: Rena Copperman
Executive Managing Editor, Juvenile: Brenda Pope-Ostrow
Editor in Chief, Juvenile: Amy Downing
Cover Crafts: Charlene Olexiewicz
Cover Photograph: Ann Bogart

Lowell House books can be purchased at special discounts when ordered in bulk for premiums and special sales. Contact Department TC at the following address:

Lowell House Juvenile
2020 Avenue of the Stars, Suite 300
Los Angeles, CA 90067

Library of Congress Catalog Card Number: 97-14876

ISBN: 1-56565-728-4

Printed in the United States of America

10 9 8 7 6 5 4 3 2

Contents

Introduction

"A friend is a present which you give yourself."

—Robert Louis Stevenson

Friendship: it means so many different things. Most importantly, friendship is a special bond that people have. Think of one of your good friends—that person you can laugh with or cry with, share secrets with, or just be yourself with—and what he or she means to you. That's what friendship is all about!

The crafts in this book will help you convey your feelings to the important people in your life. There are so many ideas to choose from, you're bound to find the perfect one. You can show your friends how much you appreciate them in a fun and creative way!

At the back of this book, you'll find instructions on how to host the ultimate craft party. Make one large craft together to symbolize the event, such as the Best Buddies' Bed Sheet on page 18 or the Keepsake Box on page 44 to hold all of your friendship mementos. Or have each friend make her own project—the Flashy Look-Alike Fashions on page 64 are great activities! A party is a perfect opportunity to share some giggles and get to know each other even better.

You'll also find loads of one-of-a-kind gifts to make for special friends. The Year of Fun calendar on page 68, the Do-It-Yourself Personalized Frame on page 56, and the Egg Carton Jewelry Box on page 30 are wonderful crafts you can personalize especially for any of your friends. They will be touched by all the thought that you put into the crafts. So put on your craft smock and get ready to choose the perfect projects for your pals in *50 Nifty Super Friendship Crafts*.

Before You Begin

The helpful hints below will make your craft-building time fun and safe for all!

♥ Adult supervision is necessary for some of the crafts, so make sure one of your parents or another adult is available to help if you choose one of the projects labeled "Adult Supervision Recommended" or "Adult Supervision Required."

♥ Read all of the directions for each craft carefully before you begin to work. Make sure you have all of the supplies you'll need, then follow the steps exactly.

♥ Think about the level of difficulty (marked in the upper right-hand corner of each craft) and the amount of time you will need to complete the project. Allow yourself plenty of time to make each craft the best you can. You don't want to be rushed or too stressed!

♥ Find a place to work that is out of the way of others and gives you room to spread out. Try to pick a place that will be easy to clean up afterward, such as a table or uncarpeted floor space. Put down newspaper or cardboard, and protect your clothing when using paint or glue.

Friendship-Power Pressed Flowers

ADULT SUPERVISION RECOMMENDED
Here's an easy way to preserve flowers so they'll last as long as your friendship!

What You'll Need

- variety of flowers
- tissue
- thick telephone book
- two bricks
- tweezers
- picture frame (any size)
- glue
- large scrap of velvet or other textured material
- scissors

Directions

1. Just before you're ready to press them, gather flowers from your yard (be sure to get a parent's permission first!), or find a field of wildflowers. Since some flowers will keep their shape and color when pressed better than others, it's best to try a variety. (Hint: Yellow and orange flowers keep their colors best.)

2. Carefully blot away any excess moisture on the flowers with a tissue.

3. Starting at least 50 pages from the front of the phone book, carefully place the flowers face down, arranging them so that they do not touch each other. You may press several flowers at once by layering them throughout the book. There should be at least 50 pages between each layer of flowers.

4. Now, close the phone book and place the two bricks on top. Leave in a dry place for four weeks. And no peeking! Opening the book before the flowers have fully dried may cause them to break. After four weeks, remove the flowers carefully. They will be very fragile and may break easily, so always handle them with tweezers.

5. Now you are ready to frame them behind glass on a textured material, such as velvet. Cut the material to fill the picture part of the frame. If necessary, glue the material down to the back of the frame. Carefully lay the flowers on top of the material. Finally, put the frame and glass over the material and flowers (just as you would with a regular photograph), and you're done!

Hanging Friendship Tree

ADULT SUPERVISION RECOMMENDED

Gather all your cards and photos from your special friends, and put them center stage! This indoor friendship tree doesn't need water—just a little TLC!

What You'll Need

- child's old umbrella (a broken one works fine)
- scissors
- three to four rolls of masking tape, various colors
- several greeting cards from friends
- photographs of you and friends together (the more the better!)
- curling ribbon, various colors
- hole punch
- heavy-duty ceiling hook

Directions

1. Begin by opening up the umbrella and carefully cutting away the fabric or plastic from the metal rods. Make sure you remove all of the material so that you're left with the "skeleton" of the umbrella.

2. Next, take the colorful masking tape and wrap it around the entire length of each rod from top to bottom. Vary the colors as you go (for instance, yellow on one, red on another, and green on the next) so that all the metal is covered.

3. Now you're ready to decorate your tree! Punch one hole in the top or corner of each greeting card and picture. Cut varying lengths of curling ribbon (one for each picture and card), pull the ribbon through each hole, and tie a knot to secure. Then, tie your treasures onto the colorful ribs of the umbrella.

4. Finally, hang your umbrella upside down on a strong ceiling hook. If your ceilings are very high, tie a ribbon to the handle of the umbrella and hang it by the ribbon rather than the handle. Now all those magic moments are on display to bring you happy memories every day!

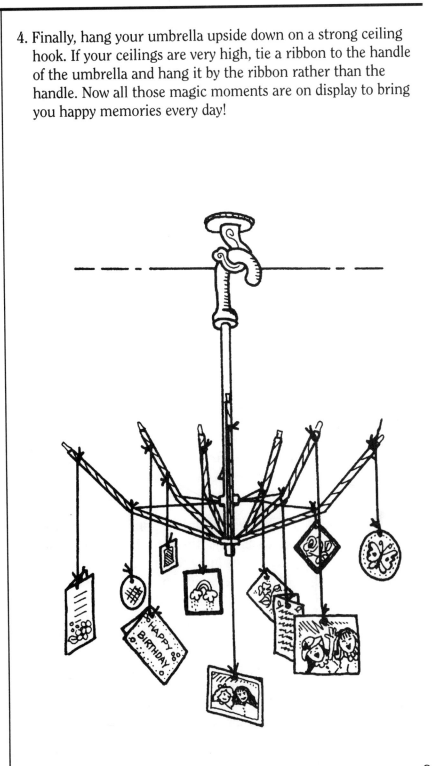

3 Get-Wired-on-Friendship Ring

A circle of colorful wires creates the perfect gift to say "You're the greatest" to a particular pal! Best of all, this gift is oh-so-easy on the pocketbook.

What You'll Need

- 10 inches of telephone cable, or other multiwire cable (most phone companies have telephone cable scraps that they give away for free)
- wire cutters
- ruler
- dresser drawer

Directions

1. With the wire cutters, strip away the outer cable covering from the wires. Then select six 10-inch wires from the group.

2. Hold the six wires in one hand, making sure that the ends you're holding are all  even. Using your ruler, measure down 4 inches and then twist all six wires one full turn so that all the wires are fastened together at the 4-inch point.

3. Shut the wires (at the 4-inch point) in a dresser drawer to hold them in place. Or, if you have a friend around, have her hold on to the ends of the wires. Ready to begin making your ring?

4. Separate the six wires into three groups of two, then braid the three sections of wires together. (If you don't know how to braid, ask a parent or older sister for help.) Continue braiding until you have 2 inches of wire braid.

5. When you're finished braiding, remove the wires from the drawer. Twist the wires that were in the drawer to the wires below the braid to form a ring. Measure it around your finger first to get an idea of how big it should be. Then, cut off the extra wire, leaving an inch of wire on either end.

6. Now you're ready to make a cool design at the top of your ring. Take each loose wire at the top (you'll have 12 in total—six from the top, six from the bottom), and separately coil each one up into a spiral design (like a snail's shell).

7. Arrange all 12 coils in an original pattern. You can lie some flat and leave others sticking up, or arrange them in a circle.

Double Layer Daisy Pin

Pin one of these flowers onto the lapel of your fave friend, and she'll be getting a gift of friendship that goes straight to the heart!

What You'll Need

- yellow, ravel-free burlap, two 2½-inch-diameter circles
- scrap of gold burlap
- white burlap (the kind that will ravel), one 1½-inch square
- scissors
- lightweight wire
- strong glue, such as rubber cement
- ½-inch-diameter flat button
- safety pin

Directions

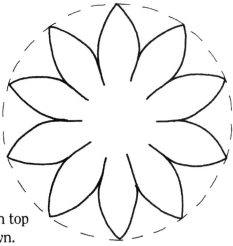

1. Cut two daisies from the yellow burlap, following the illustration here.

2. Put one set of petals over the other, staggering the petals.

3. With scissors, make two tiny slices through the center of both your daisies, one on top of the other, as shown.

4. Unravel the threads of the white burlap one at a time, in one direction only. You will have only loose threads left. Hold all the strips together in one hand and then, in the center of the strips, tie them with a small piece of lightweight wire (just once around will do the trick). These white threads will go in the center of your petals. Push the loose ends of the wire through the two tiny slices in the center of your daisies (one end through each slit) and pull tight. Twist the two wire ends together to keep the white threads securely fastened.

5. Cut out a ½-inch circle from the scrap of gold burlap and glue it to the button, completely covering it. Glue the button to the center of the white threads, as shown.

6. Finally, with a small safety pin, pin your daisy to your T-shirt and surprise someone special with your creation!

Study Buddy Book Holder

Show a friend how much you care by taking some of the pain out of homework! This super-sturdy book holder can be used time and time again.

What You'll Need

- wire coat hanger
- colorful gummed tape (gardening tape works well)
- small note card
- pen
- glue

Directions

1. Bend the wire hanger by first squeezing both arms together. Bend the two ends up and forward and fold the hook down, as shown. The hook will help support the book holder.

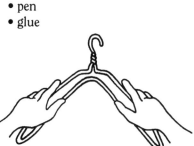

2. When the hanger is formed into the book holder shape, cover the wire completely with colorful gummed tape.

3. Now it's time to come up with a clever quote or message to write on a note card. A few examples are "Study with a Buddy," "Isn't it time for recess yet??," or "To study or not to study . . . that is the question!" Perhaps you and your friend have a secret saying or funny line between you. If so, this is a great place to put it in writing and keep it forever in her memory. Once you've scrawled your note, put some glue on the back of it and stick it to the center of the book holder. Your friendship and your secret saying will go down in the history books and live forever more!

STUDY WITH A BUDDY!

"Tied" and True Friendship Sash

ADULT SUPERVISION RECOMMENDED

A colorful sash will brighten up a best buddy's wardrobe . . . and she'll remember you fondly each and every time she ties it on!

What You'll Need

- nine pieces of colored ribbon, each 6 feet long
- dresser drawer or table and masking tape
- needle
- thread
- scissors

Directions

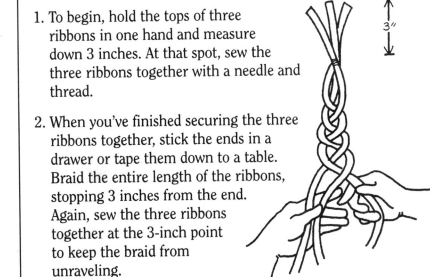

1. To begin, hold the tops of three ribbons in one hand and measure down 3 inches. At that spot, sew the three ribbons together with a needle and thread.

2. When you've finished securing the three ribbons together, stick the ends in a drawer or tape them down to a table. Braid the entire length of the ribbons, stopping 3 inches from the end. Again, sew the three ribbons together at the 3-inch point to keep the braid from unraveling.

3. Repeat this process two more times with the other six ribbons until you have three completed braids.

4. Now it's time to sew all three braids together to create the sash. To do this, hold the three braids in one hand and sew them together with a needle and thread 3 inches from one end. Then, wind the three braids around one another (about eight times) and stitch them together 3 inches from the bottom.

5. Cut the ends of the ribbon diagonally to prevent fraying and unraveling. You'll create a cool fringed look!

African Love Bead Necklace

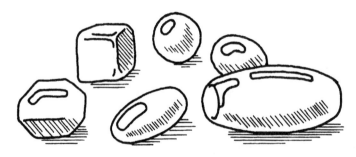

ADULT SUPERVISION REQUIRED

These tribal treasures are sure to be adored by friends anywhere around the world.

What You'll Need

- 2 cups flour
- 1 cup salt
- 1 cup water
- measuring cup
- large bowl
- toothpick
- nonstick cookie sheet
- oven mitt

- red, yellow, orange, blue, green, white, brown, and black acrylic paints
- shellac
- paintbrushes
- 24 inches of colored string or thread
- sewing needle

Directions

1. With an adult's help, preheat the oven to 325 degrees. While the oven is warming up, mix the flour and salt together in a large bowl. Then add the water a little at a time, mixing it in. If the dough is still very crumbly and dry after you've added all the water, continue adding water a teaspoon at a time until it is a doughlike consistency. Depending on how many beads you plan on making, you may need to double the recipe.

2. Knead the dough thoroughly with your hands. Continue to knead the dough until it is smooth.

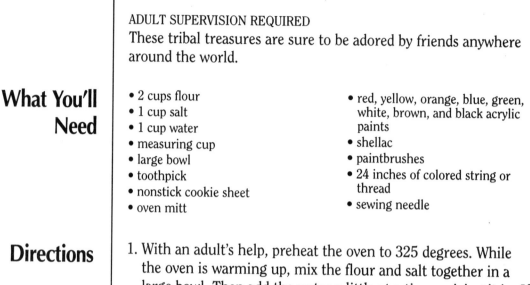

3. With the dough, begin making beads by forming small balls, about ½- to 1-inch high. Experiment with different shapes and make about 20 beads for each necklace. Make one extra-large bead that you can fit a name on.

4. Push the toothpick through the center of each bead to make a hole, then remove the toothpick to allow the bead to dry.

5. Now it's time to do the baking! Place the beads on a cookie sheet at least 1 inch apart and bake 15 to 20 minutes or until lightly browned. Using an oven mitt, remove the cookie sheet from the oven and allow the beads to cool.

6. You're ready to decorate! Paint each bead with acrylic paint. Use as many shades on each bead as you like and be creative! You can use the patterns illustrated here, or make up some of your own. Paint your friend's name or a special saying on the large bead that should fall in the center. When you're all done painting, shellac each bead and let it dry overnight.

7. With a needle, string the beads on the thread, and tie the two ends in a double knot. This ethnic-looking necklace is perfect to wear with a sweatshirt or with your favorite blouse and miniskirt.

Terrific Tees for Two

Together wherever you go! These awesome matching T-shirts will symbolize your camaraderie and show others just how much you care.

What You'll Need

- newspapers
- old clothes or paint smock
- two white, plain, oversized T-shirts
- wax paper
- acrylic paint in several of your favorite colors
- paintbrushes
- permanent ink markers

Directions

1. Slip into your old clothes or a paint smock, and head outdoors for this messy craft! Spread newspapers onto a flat surface, and lay the two T-shirts out flat, face up. Make sure you have plenty of newspapers covering the ground. Place a couple sheets of wax paper inside the shirt to prevent paint and markers from bleeding through to the other side of the shirt.

2. Dip paintbrushes into any color paint and splatter color all over the front of each one. To do this, hold the paintbrush about 3 feet over the T-shirts, and just fling your wrist. Paint will go everywhere! Use as many colors as you wish, but be sure to rinse the paintbrush with water before changing colors.

3. Let the paint dry for several hours, then turn the T-shirts over onto clean, dry newspaper. With permanent markers, write your name on the back of one T-shirt and your friend's name on the back of the other. You may want to use stencils for a neat, clean look, or write the names in your best curlicue cursive. When you're all done, you and a pal will look bold and beautiful both coming and going! (And when you are ready to wash your T-shirt, be sure to wash it by hand.)

It's a Wrap!

ADULT SUPERVISION RECOMMENDED

Your buddy will be so touched when you give her a gift that's wrapped in personalized paper that she won't even care what's inside!

What You'll Need

- several feet of white butcher paper (available at craft stores or from your local supermarket)
- poster board
- pencil
- tape
- felt markers
- glitter and sequins
- rubber cement
- scissors
- colorful ribbon

Directions

1. First, with the poster board, make a stencil that you'll repeat on the paper. In big block letters write your friend's name, ending it with a happy face, a cute heart, or other fun shape. Carefully cut out the *inside* of the letters and shape. It's okay to cut through the poster board to get to the letter—just tape it up once you've cut through it.

2. Cut the butcher paper to fit the size of the gift you'll be wrapping. On the outside of the paper (the side that will show), fill in the stencil over and over with different colored markers until the paper is filled.

3. You may want to add a special message in your own handwriting along with the stenciled name, such as "Happy Birthday, Buddy!," "Good Goin' On Your Graduation," or "Have An Awesome Holiday." When the ink is completely dry, spread clear glue on any white patches of paper, and sprinkle colorful glitter and sequins on the glue. Let it dry completely. Finally, wrap the gift and tie it all up with a ribbon!

 **Best Buddies'
Bed Sheet**

The birthday girl will have sweet dreams with this super special bed sheet that she'll treasure forever.

**What You'll
Need**

- newspapers
- white flat sheet, the same size as the birthday girl's bed
- fabric dye markers
- iron and ironing board (optional)

Directions

1. Grab a group of friends and spread out newspapers on a hard, flat surface, such as the kitchen floor. Lay the sheet over the newspapers and hand press out any creases or lumps. (If the sheet is really wrinkled, you should iron it first.)

2. Have every girl take a marker and, along the corners and edges of the sheet, scrawl a special wish that's meant exclusively for the birthday girl. Each girl can personalize her spot even more by drawing a little picture of the birthday girl doing her favorite activity (riding horses, reading books, or watching boys).

3. Then, have the girl with the prettiest handwriting write "Happy Birthday" and the date in the very center of the sheet, and draw a heart around it!

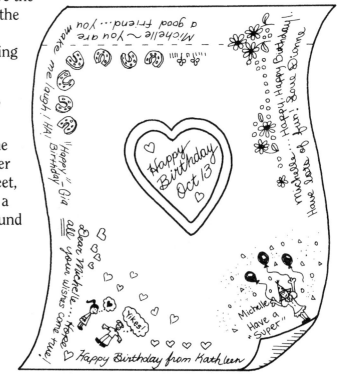

"Friends Only!" Doorknob Hanger

Adorable animal shapes are fun to paint and decorate and are the perfect addition to a buddy's bedroom.

What You'll Need

- newspapers
- 8- to 10-inch, pre-cut, wooden teddy bear, rabbit, or other animal with a hole at the top (available at craft stores)
- enamel paint, three to four colors
- paintbrushes, various sizes
- small stencils with letters or shapes, such as hearts and flowers (found at craft stores)
- thick yarn or narrow leather strip (12 to 15 inches long)

Directions

1. Spread out the newspapers over a large work surface. Choose a light-colored paint for your animal shape, and paint the front and sides all one color, using long, even strokes with one of the larger paintbrushes. Let the paint dry completely (takes about an hour), then turn over the shape and paint the back side. Let it dry as well.

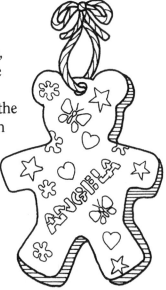

2. Now comes the fun part! Choose several stencil shapes and paint them onto the animal shape. Or, just let your imagination run wild and make up your own designs to paint on the animal. Use a variety of colors for added pizazz, or match your paint colors to your friend's room for a personal touch! (Be sure to let the front dry completely before turning it over to stencil the back.)

3. When the paint has dried thoroughly, thread the yarn or leather into the hole at the top of the hanger, make a loop large enough to fit over a doorknob, and tie it into a bow. Your special gift is now ready to be received!

Sew 'n' Sleep Autographs

ADULT SUPERVISION RECOMMENDED

It's "sew" much fun to make lasting memories with your friends. Here you can make an easy pillow to take to all your slumber parties and have everyone sign.

What You'll Need

- scissors
- ruler
- light-colored solid fabric
- printed fabric
- straight pins
- needle and thread to match fabrics
- bag of polyester stuffing
- permanent ink markers, two or three colors

Directions

1. To begin your pillow, cut out two 8-inch squares from the solid material and two 12-inch squares from the printed material. The 8-inch squares should fit inside the 12-inch squares and will be the area where your friends will sign.

2. Carefully center each of the smaller squares on the larger squares and pin them into place. With a needle and thread, sew the two smaller squares on each of the larger squares. Make your stitches about $\frac{1}{8}$ inch from the edge of each smaller square. Use small, neat stitches because they will show on your pillow.

3. Now you are ready to sew the two large squares together to form the pillow. Put the two 12-inch squares together, with the two 8-inch squares facing each other (as if the pillow were inside out). Pin the edges of the two squares together with straight pins.

4. Sew around the pillow about $\frac{1}{4}$ inch from the edge, leaving 3 to 4 inches unsewn at one corner. Then turn the pillow right side out—it should look like a flat (but still beautiful!) pillow.

5. Stuff the pillow with the polyester stuffing. Because girls will be writing on this pillow, it needs to be extra stuffed to make the material as tight as possible. Once you have stuffed the pillow, close the opening by sewing up the remaining 3 to 4 inches.

6. Here comes the fun part! Take it along to your next slumber party and have all your friends sign it using a permanent marker in one area on the light-colored fabric. Once everyone has signed it, draw a line around the group of names and date it. Then, every time you go to a slumber party (or have one of your own), you can have people sign it in another area of the pillow. What a unique collector's item!

Valentine Goodie Box

ADULT SUPERVISION RECOMMENDED

Life will be sweet for a special pal when she receives a handmade box filled with Valentine's Day goodies.

What You'll Need

- solid color contact paper in pink or red, 1 yard
- round metal cookie tin
- scissors
- white household glue
- photograph of you and a friend together
- red heart stickers
- polyurethane varnish (found at craft stores)
- flat nylon brush
- homemade or store-bought heart-shaped butter cookies
- red or pink gift ribbon
- pencil
- ruler

Directions

1. Put the cookie tin on the back side of the contact paper, and trace the outline of the cookie tin on the contact paper. Cut the paper into three strips—a wide strip for the outside of the tin, a thin strip around the lid (if even necessary), and a round piece to fit on the top of the lid.

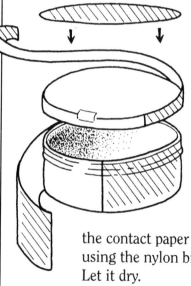

2. Carefully apply the contact paper pieces to the cookie tin. Trim off any extra paper.

3. Sparingly apply glue to the back of the picture of you and your friend. Place it on the center of the lid of the cookie tin. Add heart stickers around the photograph.

4. When the glue is dry, cover the picture, the heart stickers, and the contact paper with polyurethane varnish, using the nylon brush. Let it dry.

5. Fill the cookie tin with cookies (your friend's favorite!), and tie the ribbon around the creation. The cookies will be a quick treat, but the beautiful box will last for many happy Valentine's Days!

Baby, It's You!

ADULT SUPERVISION RECOMMENDED

All you need to make this gift a smashing success is a close connection with your pal's parents. This is one present your friend is sure to love!

What You'll Need

- snapshots of your friend (including baby photos!), ribbons or medals that she may have won, and any other meaningful mementos
- colored construction paper
- scissors
- glue
- felt tip pen
- bulletin board
- thumbtacks

Directions

1. Lay out all the photographs and materials you have collected. Cut out borders from the construction paper for each item, then glue each item onto the paper. Write a clever saying, an amusing quote, or a personal message along the top, bottom, or side of each border.

2. Cut out a circle or square from the construction paper, write your friend's name in the center, and place it in the middle of the bulletin board.

3. Decide how you want to arrange the pieces, then tack them onto the bulletin board. Play with different combinations until you're happy with the final look!

4. Arrange to take the bulletin board to your friend's house when she isn't home and hang it in her room. When she walks through the door, she'll be both surprised and delighted with this great gift!

"Members Only" Bracelet

This is a perfect bracelet to make with your favorite club buddies to prove your club is the *best!*

What You'll Need

- plastic or metal slip-on bracelet (one per friend)
- several small objects related to your club (no wider than the bracelet)
- rubber cement
- red nail polish

Directions

1. First, you need to collect or make tiny symbols or objects that represent your club. For instance, if everyone in your club loves horses, make tiny horseshoes out of clay. Or, if your club is devoted to fund-raising, collect pennies to glue on your bracelet.

2. Place the objects you've chosen or made on a table with the undersides facing up, then apply rubber cement to each object. Put the first object on the center of the bracelet. Hold it in place for several minutes to make sure it sticks.

3. Continue gluing on one object at a time, working outward toward the ends, until you've used all the objects or run out of room on the bracelet. Let the bracelet dry overnight in a cool place.

4. When the glue is completely dry and the objects are secure, print the club's secret password with red nail polish on the inside of the bracelet. Let it dry. This fine jewelry is now fit for wearing with friends—and only you and the other club members know the secret password!

Quick 'n' Easy Ring

ADULT SUPERVISION RECOMMENDED

This traditional friendship ring takes less than five minutes to make!

What You'll Need

- plain key ring (small enough to fit around your ring finger)
- two pieces of six-ply embroidery thread, 15 inches long (two different colors—you and your best friend's favorites)
- scissors
- rubber cement

Directions

1. Lay the two pieces of thread side by side, and flatten them out with your hand. Hold the ends of the threads on the key ring with your thumb, and with the other hand, begin wrapping the strands around the ring in a slightly diagonal direction.

2. Continue wrapping the thread all the way around the key ring, keeping the threads flat against the ring. Make sure the colors are wound tightly together so that the key ring doesn't show through.

3. When you get to the end, wrap over the loose ends (the ones under your thumb) so that the strands are secure. Then wrap the threads around two to three times more and tie a small knot. To keep the ends in place, brush on a little rubber cement.

One Step Further

Because these rings are so thin, you can wear two or three on one finger. Make several rings in the same colors or use different shades for a cool effect!

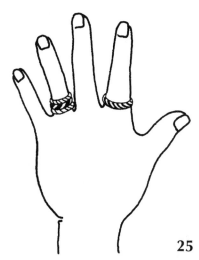

Makin' Memories Diary

ADULT SUPERVISION RECOMMENDED

Any pal would flip over this handmade diary—a special spot to scribble down secret thoughts!

What You'll Need

- two pieces of gray construction paper
- rubber cement
- scissors
- two pieces of heavy, 6-by-9-inch cardboard
- decorative piece of floral paper (like wrapping paper)
- hole punch
- ruler
- pencil
- eraser
- stack of 6-by-9-inch writing paper
- piece of string or twine, 15 inches long

Directions

1. Cut two rectangles of construction paper, each 7 inches by 10 inches. Spread the glue evenly onto the back of one of the pieces, and apply a piece of the 6-by-9-inch cardboard to the center of the paper. Wrap the ½-inch border of the paper around the sides so that the cardboard front and sides are completely covered. You may have to apply more glue to get the corners to stay down. Repeat the same process with the second piece of cardboard and construction paper. These pieces are the front and back covers of your diary.

2. Cut the decorative floral paper approximately 4 inches by 7 inches so that it fits onto the front cover as shown, then glue it into place.

3. Now it's time to punch holes in the covers of the diary. On both pieces of cardboard, measure ¾ inch from their left sides. With a ruler, draw a faint pencil line down the length of the book at the ¾-inch point. Now, measure 2 inches from the bottom of the cardboard and mark an X on the line. Measure 3 inches above that and mark another X. Finally, measure up 2 inches and draw an X. Do this on both the front and back covers.

4. Stack the two pieces of cardboard together with the X's running down the left side on the front cover. Make sure that the X's on the front cover match up exactly with the X's on the back cover.

When you're certain that you've measured correctly, punch holes over all the X's with the hole punch. Erase any visible pencil markings.

5. Place the stack of 6-by-9-inch paper between the two pieces of cardboard so that the left sides of the paper are even with the left sides of the covers.

6. Next, stick the pencil inside the holes in the cardboard, and draw three little circles onto the paper where you'll punch the holes. This step is tricky since you must hold the stack of paper and cardboard completely still as you make your markings. When your markings are accurate, punch holes in the paper. If the hole punch won't go through the whole stack, punch fewer sheets at a time, but make sure all the holes are in the same location.

7. Now you are ready to loosely string together the diary. Take your piece of twine and tie a double knot in the end. Starting from the back side, string the twine up through the bottom hole and come down through the next set of holes. Pull the twine back up through the top and final hole. Tie a double knot directly over the hole so that the string won't slip through. Don't string it too tightly; otherwise, the front cover may be difficult to open. You can leave the long pieces hanging or cut them off—it's up to you! Now, you've got a totally handmade treasure that's perfect for your pal's most personal pennings!

Friends Forever Anklet

Get your friendship started on the right foot with this adorable anklet.

What You'll Need

- three pieces of thick yarn (three different colors), 12 inches each
- tape
- five to eight small beads (with holes big enough for two pieces of yarn to fit through)
- ruler

Directions

1. Lay out the three pieces of yarn side by side. Measure down 2 inches from the top of the yarn and tie a knot. Tape the ends down on a table to keep the anklet in place while you're braiding. Begin braiding the yarn and continue for an inch.

2. Then thread two of the strands through one bead—it doesn't matter which two you thread through the bead. Braid down another inch and thread another bead through two strands. Continue this same pattern until you've braided and beaded about 6 inches of the yarn.

3. Measure the creation around your ankle to make sure it's the appropriate size. If it's too long, undo some of the braid; if it's too short, add more braiding and beads.

4. When your anklet is the correct size, remove the anklet from the table, and tie a knot at both ends to keep the yarn from coming undone. Wrap it around your ankle, and tie the ends into a bow or a loose knot. Cut off any loose ends. Now, make one for your pal, and you'll have a symbol of friendship you'll never walk away from!

Nature's Own Bookmark

ADULT SUPERVISION RECOMMENDED

Bring a bit of the great outdoors into your buddy's latest reading assignment with this "natural" bookmark!

What You'll Need

- construction paper
- ruler
- scissors
- pressed flowers, seeds, or leaves
- glue
- clear, self-stick paper (found at craft stores)
- hole punch
- ribbon or yarn

Directions

1. Cut a piece of construction paper about 7 inches long and 2 inches wide. Use a ruler to make the edges straight.

2. Glue the pressed flowers, seeds, or leaves onto the paper. (Learn how to make your own pressed flowers on page 3.)

3. Cut two pieces of self-stick clear paper the same size as the construction paper. Peel off the backing and put one piece on the back of the bookmark and one piece on the front so that the decorations are covered.

4. Punch a hole in the top with a hole punch. Put several strands of ribbon or yarn through the hole, and tie each one individually around the hole. What a way to mark the spot!

 **Egg Carton Jewelry Box**

This box is "eggs-ceptionally" unusual and creative—and a fun way for a friend to store her treasures!

What You'll Need

- newspapers
- empty egg carton, foam or cardboard
- poster paint
- paintbrush
- photographs (optional)
- ribbon pieces and fake jewels
- 12 cotton balls
- glue

Directions

1. Spread the newspaper over a large work surface. Paint the entire egg carton with poster paint, and let it dry completely.

2. Decorate the outside of the box with ribbons and jewels. (You can even glue on pictures of you and your friends!)

3. Open up the box, and place a small amount of glue in the bottom of each egg section. Then put a cotton ball in each one. Now you've got a great resting place for jewelry!

Bloomin' Buddy Box

A healthy, thriving plant is the gift of choice since you can watch it grow along with your friendship! Plant it inside this handmade basket for a lasting (and living!) present.

What You'll Need

- newspaper
- plastic berry basket
- two yards of ½-inch-wide ribbon
- aluminum foil
- garden soil
- small plant

Directions

1. Spread the newspaper over a large work surface. Take the berry basket and weave the ribbon in and out of the basket holes as shown, leaving enough ribbon at each end so that you can tie a bow when you're finished weaving.

2. Line the entire basket (including the sides) with two layers of aluminum foil. Lay the foil so that the shiny side faces the basket holes.

3. Fill the lined basket with garden soil and then put in a small plant. Make sure you get the roots embedded deeply into the soil. Add water and get ready to make a special delivery!

One Step Further

Write a special message on a note card, punch it with a hole punch, and use some leftover ribbon to attach it to the basket. On the bottom of the note card, include simple instructions on how to care for the plant.

Heart-to-Heart Pin

Talk about wearing your heart on your sleeve! "Doughn't" ya know this heart pin is the perfect way to say "You're special" to a favorite friend?

What You'll Need

- slice of white bread
- 1 teaspoon white glue
- 1 teaspoon water
- heart-shaped cookie cutter
- safety pin
- red and white enamel paint
- paintbrush

Directions

1. First, remove the crust from the slice of bread. Then pour a teaspoon of glue and a teaspoon of water over the bread.

2. Here comes the fun part: Knead the bread between your palms until it's no longer sticky. Set the dough aside, and wash your hands thoroughly.

3. Using your hand and a flat surface, press the dough to ¼-inch thickness. Cut out a heart shape with the cookie cutter. Depending on the size of the cookie cutter, you may be able to cut out two shapes from the bread. Store the remaining dough in the refrigerator in an airtight plastic bag. It will last a couple of days.

4. Set your heart shape in a safe, dry place, and leave it to harden for 48 hours.

5. When 48 hours have passed, pinch off a pea-sized piece of the dough that was stored in the refrigerator. This piece will be used to hold the safety pin in place, which will hold your pin in place! Press the little ball of dough between your palms into a very thin oval shape, small enough to fit onto the center back of your heart.

6. Now cover one side of the oval with glue. Lay the safety pin across the center back of your heart, and lay the oval shape over one side of the safety pin as shown. Be sure that the safety pin can still open. Let it dry for several hours.

7. Once the safety pin has dried in place, paint the front of your heart red. Let the paint dry completely (about an hour or two), then paint your friend's name in white over the red. Now you've got a heartfelt gift to give that's sure to be admired by all!

One Step Further

Now that you know how to make a heart pin from bread and glue, how about trying some different shapes? Stars, flowers, four-leaf clovers, and animals are just a few of the pin shapes you can make.

Hassle-Free Headbands for Two

What You'll Need

ADULT SUPERVISION RECOMMENDED
Get together with a friend, then put your two heads together to whip up a set of matching headbands.

- 2 yards of 1½-inch velvet ribbon in your favorite color
- 12 small, fake pearls
- needle and thread (same color as the velvet)

- strong glue
- iron and ironing board
- scissors

Directions

1. You'll have enough supplies to make two headbands, so cut the 2 yards of velvet ribbon in half and split the pearls between you and your pal. Before cutting the velvet, measure it around your head by placing the ribbon under your hair at the nape of the neck and tying it into a bow at the top of your head as shown. Cut it only when you've determined how long you want the headband to be. Then untie the bow for the next step.

2. Hem under the two ends of the velvet ribbon so that they won't fray and come unraveled. Turn each side under about ¼ inch and iron into place. With the needle and thread, sew down each side, taking care to use short, neat, and accurate stitches.

3. Glue three pearls on each end of your headband, in any arrangement you like. Let the glue dry for several hours before tying on your newest creation sensation!

One Step Further

Got some extra velvet ribbon? Try using the same instructions to make matching chokers or bracelets, and you'll really double your fashion pleasure!

Forever Fresh!

These beautiful and easy-to-make pomander balls used to freshen drawers and closets have a lovely scent and will last years into your friendship.

What You'll Need

- large orange
- box of whole cloves
- velvet ribbon
- several straight pins

Directions

1. Begin sticking the cloves into the orange, putting them right next to each other. It will take patience to get the whole orange completely covered, but once you're done, the pomander ball will last for many years. And don't worry about the orange spoiling! The cloves will protect the fruit and keep it fresh.

2. Wrap velvet ribbon around the orange. Tie a loop at the top, so your friend can hang it in her closet. Insert straight pins into the ribbon to keep it in place.

3. When you give the gift, let your friend know that this gift will keep moths away and is therefore perfect for putting in a drawer with wool garments.

Official Initial Charm Bracelet

ADULT SUPERVISION REQUIRED

Your friends will be "charmed" when you suggest making these bracelets to have as keepsakes.

What You'll Need

- mixing bowl
- 1 cup cornstarch
- 1 cup salt
- cooking pot
- ½ cup water
- rolling pin
- stirring spoon
- several sharp knives
- toothpicks
- nonstick cookie sheet
- colorful tempera paints
- oven mitt
- paintbrushes
- pencil
- scissors
- shoestrings
- permanent markers
- colorful thread

Directions

1. With an adult's help, preheat the oven to 300 degrees. While the oven is heating up, make the dough for the charms. In the mixing bowl, combine the cornstarch and salt. Have an adult help you bring the water to a boil in a pot on the stove. Then lower the temperature to medium heat and slowly stir the cornstarch and salt mixture into the water. Stir the mixture until it becomes stiff. Remove the pot from the heat, and let it cool slightly. Knead the warm dough until it has a smooth consistency.

2. With a rolling pin, roll the dough to a thickness of about ⅛ inch. Divide the dough equally among your pals. Each friend will make a charm for each person in the group, including herself. Each charm should be about the size of a penny. With a knife, cut out the charms into hearts, stars, circles, or any other small, fun shapes. Using a toothpick, poke a small hole near the top of each charm large enough to poke the thread through.

3. Use a toothpick to inscribe your initials on one side and your birth date on the other. If the dough becomes crumbly, try gently smoothing it with your fingers.

4. Now you are ready to dry the charms. Put them on the cookie sheet, separated from each other. Place the cookie sheet in a 300-degree oven for about 10 to 15 minutes. Take out the cookie sheet using the oven mitt, and allow the charms to cool.

5. Give each friend the charms she made, as well as a different color of paint, so that each friend can paint them all one color. When the charms have dried, everyone keeps one of the charms and gives one to each friend in the group.

6. Now give a shoestring to each of your pals. Each girl needs to make a small loop at one end of the shoelace, by wrapping it around the pencil, then knotting it off. Make two or three tight knots so that the loop will remain tied.

7. Slip the shoelace off the pencil. Snip the plastic tip off the shoelace very close to where you tied the knots.

8. Measure the length of the bracelet by marking where the loop meets the shoelace when wrapped around your wrist.

9. Tie a knot about ½ inch from the mark on the shoelace. Keep knotting in the same spot, making the knot bigger and bigger. You'll know the knot is the right size when it can barely squeeze through the loop. This will make the bracelet easy to put on and take off. Snip the long end off. You've now created a bracelet with a built-in fastener.

10. Decorate your bracelet with markers. You can make stripes or solids, or draw rainbows or hearts—let your imagination run wild!

11. Now sew the bracelet charms on just as you would a button. Each charm represents one of your friends, and together they symbolize a whole rainbow of friendships!

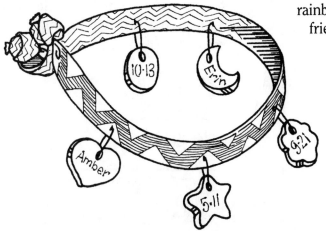

Forever Friendship Flowers

ADULT SUPERVISION RECOMMENDED

Roses and carnations that won't ever wilt, die, or fade—what a perfect way to say, "I hope our friendship blossoms forever!"

What You'll Need

- colored facial tissue
- pipe cleaners
- small pair of scissors
- lipstick

Directions

1. Hold the center of one tissue between your fingers and shake it downward. With your other hand, wind a pipe cleaner around the center of the tissue just below your fingers. The pipe cleaner will be the "stem" of the flower.

2. Using a small pair of scissors, cut the corners of the tissue to make rounded petals for roses. For carnations, snip the edge of the tissue to make fringelike petals.

3. Holding the stem, turn the tissue upward. Brush the flower petals with lipstick from about an inch inside the flower to the edge. Don't press down hard with the lipstick— brush lightly for just a touch of color.

One Step Further

Gather several shades of lipstick and make a dozen tissue flowers, then color each one a different shade. Place the flowers into a small vase, then spritz the bouquet with your favorite perfume. Your paper creation will look and smell like the real thing!

Pocket Pal
File Holder

ADULT SUPERVISION RECOMMENDED

When you want to store precious memories, these secret pouches do it all!

What You'll Need

- notebook, 8½ by 11 inches, about 30 pages
- glue
- felt tip marker
- wrapping paper with print or design
- scissors
- two pieces of velvet ribbon, each 8 inches long

Directions

1. First, you want to create pockets in your notebook. Open up the book to pages 1 and 2. On the back side of page 1, apply glue in a straight line across the top, bottom, and inside of the page. Press it to the second page. When the glue dries, you'll have a "pocket" in the center. Repeat this with pages 3 and 4, 5 and 6, and so on, until you have 15 pockets in the notebook.

2. Go through the notebook and mark specific special events on each envelope. ("Disneyland Memorabilia," "12th Birthday Party," and "5th Grade Memories" are a few examples.) If you're giving this gift to a friend, label the pouches with special experiences you've shared. It's the perfect spot for storing all those outrageous memories! You can also use this book as a diary to record special events and precious moments.

3. Before you start filling up the file holder, decorate the cover and back cover. Take the wrapping paper (your choice—wild and bright, or soft and feminine!) and trace the cover and back cover onto the blank side of the paper. Then cut the two pieces out and glue them to the front and back covers. Trim off any extra paper. Finally, take the two ribbons, and glue one to the center of the back cover and the other to the center of the front cover. Tie a knot in the end of each ribbon to prevent fraying. Then use these ribbons to "tie up" your best-kept secrets!

 # Secret Message Seashell Earrings

These seashell earrings are an ocean of fun to wear and a cinch to make!

What You'll Need

- two corkscrew-type seashells, no bigger than 2 or 2½ inches (if you don't live near the ocean, craft stores carry a wide variety of seashells)
- strong glue
- tweezers
- two earring clips (available at drug, discount, and craft stores)
- two 1½-inch pieces of paper
- pen

Directions

1. Wash the seashells and dry them thoroughly. Put them on a table with the back sides facing up. Squeeze a few drops of strong-holding glue onto the backs of the shells.

2. Using the tweezers, pick up the shells one at a time and place them very gently on top of the earring clips, right in the center. Let the glue dry for several hours.

3. While the glue is drying, take the tiny pieces of paper and write secret notes for your friend's eyes (and ears!) only. Then roll them up into small, tight cylinders.

4. Once the earrings have dried, carefully stick the notes into the two shells, and give them to your friend. If the notes don't fit in the shells, make them even smaller!

The Lantern of Friendship

ADULT SUPERVISION REQUIRED

Got a radiant relationship you're excited about? Let the light of friendship shine with this candle holder.

What You'll Need

- empty, smooth-sided tin can, at least 7 inches high and 4¼ inches in diameter
- paper
- pencil
- permanent marking pen
- assorted sizes of nails
- hammer
- short, thick candle
- match

Directions

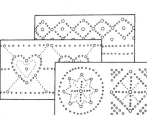

1. Clean the inside of the can and remove the paper label and glue.

2. On a scratch piece of paper, create a design that can go all around the can. Some examples are shown. Then draw the design on the can with a permanent marker.

3. Fill the can with water and put it into the freezer until the water is frozen solid. This will help the can hold its shape when you make it into a lantern.

4. Now, with the hammer and nails, punch holes in the can along the design you drew. Use an assortment of different-sized nails to enhance your design. Leave at least ¼ inch between the holes. Be sure to have an adult supervise. If the ice starts melting, put it back in the freezer for a while.

5. When you're done punching the holes, get the ice out of the can by melting it under hot water.

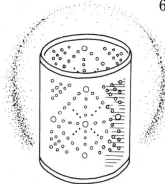

6. Dry out the can, then stick a short candle in the bottom. Make sure the candle is wide enough so that it can stand on its own. With an adult's help, light the candle, then turn down the lights and admire your beautiful lantern!

ADULT SUPERVISION RECOMMENDED

Say hello to a best buddy with this cantaloupe seed necklace, which is an awesome replica of the traditional Hawaiian friendship necklace.

What You'll Need

- seeds from four or five cantaloupes
- fine mesh sieve
- paper towels
- package of dark brown water dye
- plastic container for the dye
- hot water
- newspapers
- nylon sewing thread or a package of bead-stringing thread
- scissors
- felt marking pen
- needle
- five to seven brown, white, gray, or brightly colored beads, ¼- to ⅜-inch in diameter
- ruler

Directions

1. Remove the seeds from the cantaloupes (you and a pal can share the tasty fruit and store the remaining cantaloupe in the refrigerator!), and put the seeds into a sieve to be washed. Make sure there are no small pieces of melon remaining. Then spread the seeds out in a single layer on paper towels to dry.

2. Put 1 tablespoon of dark brown dye in a plastic container, and add 2 tablespoons of hot water. Stir the mixture to melt the dye. Then, when the dye has dissolved, add ½ cup more hot water and stir. Add ⅓ cup of seeds to the dye, stir well, and let them soak for an hour.

3. When the seeds are dark, pour the contents of the plastic container (seeds and dye) into the sieve over the sink. Rinse out the sink right away so that the dye doesn't stain it. Rinse the seeds first with hot water, then with cold water.

4. Lay down newspapers over a work surface, and lay paper towels on top of the newspaper. Put the seeds in a single layer on top of the paper towels to dry.

5. Hold the thread around your neck to measure how long you want the necklace to be. (Make sure it's long enough to go over your head.) Add 2 inches of extra thread at each end and cut.

6. Lay out the thread and mark the center with the felt marker. Plan where you want to add the beads (one for every 2 or 3 inches of cantaloupe seeds, for instance), and mark the thread with a pen. Also, mark the thread 2 inches from each end.

7. Thread the needle with the marked thread, and tie a knot 2 inches in from one end of the thread (at the pen mark). Now, push the needle through the flat center of each seed at the broadest point, and pull the thread through. Pull the seed down to the knot, and continue threading seeds. When you reach a pen mark, add a bead, then continue adding the seeds. (The seeds will hold the beads in place. If the hole of a bead is larger than the seed, then you need to find smaller beads.)

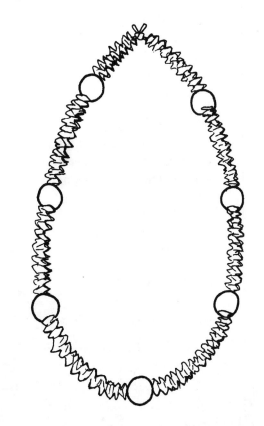

8. When you have filled the thread with seeds and beads and have reached the mark 2 inches from the end, remove the needle from the thread. Tie a knot at the 2-inch mark, then tie the two ends together in a knot. Cut off the extra thread and you're now ready to present your version of an authentic Hawaiian friendship necklace!

Keepsake Box

Need a holding place for all those special souvenirs? This box is the perfect place for storing ticket stubs, private notes, pictures, and anything else you hold near and dear to your heart!

What You'll Need

- empty shoe box with lid
- colorful wrapping paper, pages from your favorite magazine, and wallet-size pictures of you and a best buddy

- scissors
- glue
- shellac
- paintbrush

Directions

1. The design on the outside of this box should be an expression of you, so tap into your creative talents! Begin by cutting squares and rectangles of various sizes from wrapping paper and magazine pages. Cut enough to cover the outside of both the lid and the box.

2. Attach the lid to the box by slicing the two back corners of the lid up the corner creases, as shown. Then, spread glue across the entire lip of the lid, from one sliced corner to the other. Press it firmly to the shoe box. Now you should be able to lift the lid and close it like a jewelry box.

3. Glue the paper, magazine pages, and wallet-size pictures onto the box and lid. Be creative! Glue some pictures upside down, some sideways, and some overlapping others. The crazier the better! After all, it's an extension of you!

4. When the entire box and lid are covered, paint the box with shellac and let it dry completely. Give your treasure to a true friend or keep it for your own use!

Great Grains Friendship Vase

ADULT SUPERVISION REQUIRED
This unique vase deserves a place of honor in your best buddy's bedroom!

What You'll Need

- soap
- paper towels
- newspapers
- glass jar (such as a mayonnaise jar)
- 2 cups uncooked white rice
- glue stick

- rubber cement
- spray paint, in earthy colors such as rust, gold, and brown
- dried flower arrangement
- felt markers (optional)
- nail polish (optional)

Directions

1. Remove any labels from the jar and wash it with soap and water. Then dry it thoroughly with paper towels.

2. Spread newspapers on a large work surface. On one part of the newspaper, spread out the rice. With the glue stick, spread glue all over the outside of the glass jar. Work quickly so that the glue doesn't dry! Roll the glue-covered jar in the rice. Let it dry.

3. In case you missed any spots, spread another coat of glue on the jar, and roll it again in the rice, this time making sure that all areas of the jar get covered. If you are having problems getting the rice to stick in some areas, dab those places with rubber cement and then roll it in the rice. Allow it to dry.

4. With a parent's help, spray the entire jar with paint. You can also use felt markers or nail polish to create shapes or designs if you don't want to paint the whole vase one color.

5. When the paint or polish has dried, arrange a bouquet of dried flowers in the vase. Tell your friend to keep the jar dry at all times since water may loosen the glue.

ADULT SUPERVISION RECOMMENDED
This decorative paper chain will link together your group of friends in a very special way.

What You'll Need

- construction paper in assorted colors
- ruler
- scissors
- felt tip pens in assorted colors
- stapler

Directions

1. With a group of friends, measure and cut strips of construction paper 6 inches long by 2 inches wide. Each girl in the group should have the same number of strips as there are girls involved. For instance, if there are six girls at the party, each girl should have six strips.

2. When the party begins, ask each friend to write her name on all the strips of construction paper, which will later be the chain links. When everyone is done, have the girls trade their pieces of paper with each other. Each girl should end up with a paper link from each of the girls, as well as still have one of her own.

3. Now comes the fun part! Each player writes a special message to the girl whose name is on each paper link. (This means she will also be writing a message to herself.) The message should be written on the side opposite the name. It can be something the player admires about her, a special secret only for her, or an inspirational saying. Once a message has been written, "lock" the link by looping the paper into a circle and stapling the ends together. The name of the girl should be on the outside of the link.

4. When all of the links have been locked, they should be returned to their original owner (the girl whose name is written on the links). Then, with additional paper strips, each girl can put her links together, building a whole chain, as shown in the illustration on the following page.

5. Now tell each girl to take her chain home, and when she is feeling down, she can tear off one of the chains with her name on it. When she reads the special message from a good friend, it's sure to give her a lift!

One Step Further

You can make one of these chains of friendship for an extra-special friend by writing happy thoughts and encouraging words on several different links. This is one chain that won't weigh anybody down!

Pasta Necklace

Try this "tasteful" addition to your favorite friend's funky jewelry collection—a pasta necklace!

What You'll Need

- nylon fishing line or heavy string
- scissors
- pasta with holes (all different shapes, sizes, and colors)
- several wooden and gold beads
- shellac
- paintbrush

Directions

1. Hold the nylon fishing line or string around your neck to measure the appropriate length before cutting. A good length is usually 24 to 36 inches. Cut it, then lay the fishing line or string out in front of you.

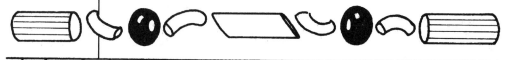

2. Set the pasta pieces you plan to use next to the fishing line or string, and arrange them in a fun pattern. Separate every third or fourth pasta piece with a bead. Play with the combinations, until you come up with a pattern that you love!

3. String on the pasta and beads in the pattern you've created. Don't forget to leave about 2 inches on either side of the line, so when you've finished stringing, you can tie the two ends of the necklace into a tight knot.

4. Paint the necklace with a thin coat of shellac to make it shine. Once one side is dry, paint the other side. After that side has dried, put it on and show it off!

One Step Further

You're sure to have leftover pasta, so if you've got some more beads, try making a bracelet or even a thin belt in the same pattern.

Fabulous Felt Friendship Patches

ADULT SUPERVISION REQUIRED
What a heart-*felt* way to say you care.

What You'll Need

- iron-on felt material, in several colors (sold at craft stores in square sheets)
- paper figures to trace, such as a bicyclist, tennis player, or cheerleader (available at craft and hobby stores)

- scissors
- felt tip pen
- iron and ironing board
- plain T-shirt

Directions

1. The first step is to choose the symbols that represent you and your friend. Since you'll be applying these to a plain T-shirt, pick several figures so that you can iron on more than one design. Come up with some of your own designs and figures.

2. Once you've decided on a theme, place the paper figure on top of the iron-on felt, and carefully trace around the edges using a felt tip pen. Use a light hand so that the ink won't spread. Cut out the designs.

3. Follow the manufacturer's instructions for using the iron-on felt when applying it to the T-shirt. Handle the iron with care—and only under the supervision of an adult. You can apply the patches on the front, on the back, or on both sleeves for extra flair. Whichever way you choose, your pal is sure to be delighted!

49

Lace Barrette

ADULT SUPERVISION RECOMMENDED
Update and upgrade a tired steel barrette for a feminine look a
friend will never forget.

What You'll Need

- steel hair barrette
- rubber cement
- lace, 12 to 15 inches long
- scissors
- super glue (or other very strong glue)
- about a dozen small fake pearls

Directions

1. Open the barrette. Apply a small amount of rubber cement to the wrong side of the lace (too much glue will ruin the lace!), and apply it to the underside of the top part of the barrette.

2. Wrap the lace around the length of the barrette until the top of the barrette is covered. Carefully glue down the end of the lace and let it dry.

3. Now, squeeze a dot of super glue onto each pearl, and apply them around the outside edges of the barrette, creating a border. You'll have to hold each pearl to the lace for about a minute to make sure the glue has dried. Let the glue dry overnight, and the next day, your barrette with the feminine touch is ready to be worn and adored!

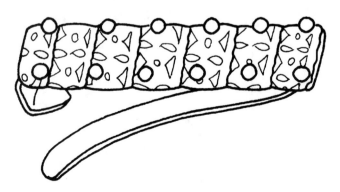

Frame Your Feelings!

ADULT SUPERVISION REQUIRED
Take a special card or poem and frame it, creating an old-fashioned, charming look.

What You'll Need

- a new or old card with a special poem or message
- scissors
- matches
- white household glue

- 5-by-7-inch matte board
- polyurethane varnish
- paintbrush
- 5-by-7-inch frame, with a stand on the back

Directions

1. Cut the card in half and keep the side with the poem or message printed on it. Ask an adult to help you burn the edges of the card with a match. *Do not do this step alone!* Over a sink, carefully burn away the outside edges of the card without burning the words. Once you light the match, be ready to blow it out immediately since all you want is a slightly burnt look around the edges.

2. Glue the card onto the center of the matte board, then brush on a layer of the polyurethane varnish. Let it dry for an hour, then brush on another coat. Let it dry overnight.

3. Slip the board inside the frame, and the piece is ready for display!

One Step Further

For an even more personalized touch, sign the card before you burn the edges. Or, paint your name and your friend's name on the glass of the frame with puffy paints, which can be found in any craft store.

Folded Paper Gift Box

When you give a friend a special small gift, deliver it to her in this beautiful box she'll treasure.

What You'll Need

- one sheet of medium-weight paper, 8½ inches square
- one sheet of medium-weight paper, 8¾ inches square
- markers, various colors
- stickers (optional)
- scissors
- several cotton balls
- ribbon

Directions

1. The first step is to decorate both sheets of paper however you wish. You can cover it with fun stickers or draw all sorts of fun designs on it. Another option is to use heavy wrapping paper with some kind of printed pattern.

2. Make the open box using the sheet of 8½-inch square paper. To do this, fold the paper diagonally in half, first one way and then the other. Make firm creases in the folds so that you can easily tell where the paper has been folded once you open it. Unfold the paper.

3. Fold all four corners so that they meet at the center point, then unfold the paper.

4. Now, fold each corner to the crease lines that you just made in step 3. Unfold the paper.

5. One by one, fold the corners so that they meet the crease lines on the opposite side of the square, as illustrated. Again, unfold the paper.

6. Your paper should now look like this. Cut the paper along the thick lines indicated in the illustration.

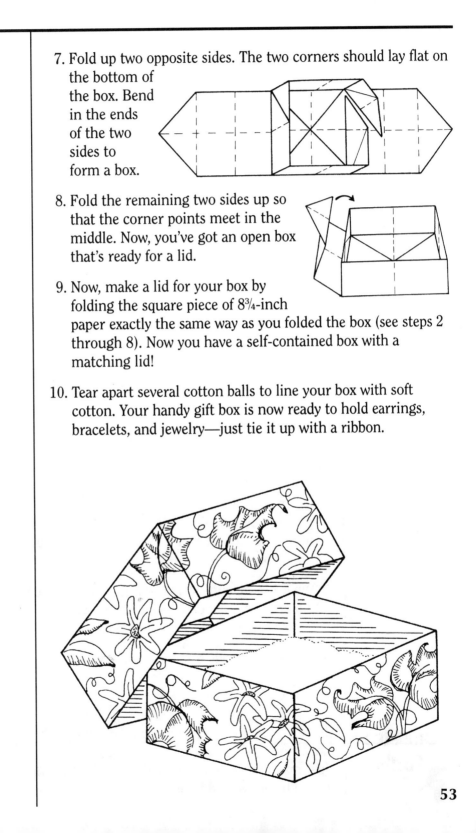

7. Fold up two opposite sides. The two corners should lay flat on the bottom of the box. Bend in the ends of the two sides to form a box.

8. Fold the remaining two sides up so that the corner points meet in the middle. Now, you've got an open box that's ready for a lid.

9. Now, make a lid for your box by folding the square piece of 8¾-inch paper exactly the same way as you folded the box (see steps 2 through 8). Now you have a self-contained box with a matching lid!

10. Tear apart several cotton balls to line your box with soft cotton. Your handy gift box is now ready to hold earrings, bracelets, and jewelry—just tie it up with a ribbon.

Secret Code Bracelet

All friends share classified information! Check out this cryptic way to forever document your best-kept secrets.

- plastic square beads containing letters of the alphabet (found at craft stores)
- one shoelace in a bright color or neon pattern, at least 8 to 10 inches long
- several small plastic beads with holes big enough to fit the shoelace through

Directions

1. The first step is to plan your secret message so that you can spell out the code. The code will consist of the first letters of each word. For example, "Happy Birthday To A Wild Girl" would be HBTAWG, or "Janette And Jennifer Best Buds For Life" would be JAJBBFL. (Imagine how much fun it'll be to keep your message a secret while everyone tries to guess the meaning!)

2. Once you've decided on a message, string the letters in the correct order onto the shoelace. (The plastic ends of the shoelace should make it easy for you to string the beads.) Center the letters in the middle of the shoelace, then add beads in any color or pattern you choose on either side of the message. You don't need to fill the lace with beads, especially if the shoelace is a fun color.

3. When you're done stringing the beads or when you have about 2 inches left on either end of the shoelace, tie a knot at each end so that the beads won't slip off.

4. Now you're ready to tie the bracelet onto your friend's wrist. The shoelace material will easily hold a knot, but it will still be easy enough to untie when you're ready to remove the bracelet.

One Step Further

To add real pizazz to this bracelet, purchase a bracelet clasp at the craft store and tie it onto the ends instead of relying on a knot. Just make sure you measure the length of the bracelet on your friend before you add the clasp.

Buddy-Up Buttons

ADULT SUPERVISION RECOMMENDED

Turn boring buttons into beautiful ones, and make a matching set for a pal!

What You'll Need

- blouse with buttons that have loops in the back (the kinds with holes won't work!)
- scissors
- variety of fabric scraps
- fabric glue
- needle
- thread

Directions

1. Pick a blouse or shirt from your closet that you want updated, and carefully remove the buttons by snipping threads with the scissors. (Check with a parent before setting the scissors to a blouse you shouldn't!)

2. Choose the fabric to cover the buttons. You can cover each button in a different fabric, or for a more conservative look, choose the same fabric for all the buttons.

3. Lay each button facedown on the wrong side the fabric, and cut the material into a circle that's about $1\frac{1}{2}$ inches wider than the button.

4. Spread the wrong side of the fabric with glue, making sure you cover the entire circle. Wrap the material around the button, pressing out any creases and making sure the fabric is flat against the button. Glue the ends to the underside of the button, but don't cover the loop. If necessary, trim off some of the excess material and threads.

5. Repeat steps 3 and 4 until you have covered all the buttons.

6. When the glue has dried on all the buttons, sew the new buttons onto your blouse. Then, make a matching set for a friend for double the fashion fun!

Do-It-Yourself Personalized Frame

ADULT SUPERVISION REQUIRED
Create an original frame that can be personalized for any special friend.

What You'll Need

- foam-core board
- X-Acto knife
- thick ribbon, lace, or other material
- fabric glue
- buttons, rhinestones, or any other odds and ends
- picture of you and a friend

Directions

1. First, you need to cut out your frame and its back. With an X-Acto knife and a parent's help, cut two foam-core rectangles that are an inch taller and wider than the picture you will be using. For instance, if the picture you want to use is 3½ by 5 inches, cut two rectangles 4½ by 6 inches.

2. With one rectangle, draw a smaller rectangle inside it that is ½ inch smaller all the way around. Then ask a parent to help you cut out the smaller rectangle. This is where your picture will fit.

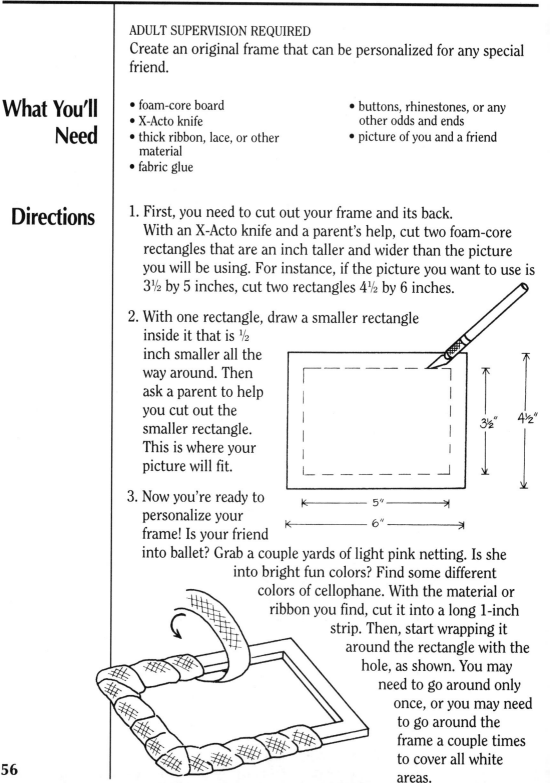

3. Now you're ready to personalize your frame! Is your friend into ballet? Grab a couple yards of light pink netting. Is she into bright fun colors? Find some different colors of cellophane. With the material or ribbon you find, cut it into a long 1-inch strip. Then, start wrapping it around the rectangle with the hole, as shown. You may need to go around only once, or you may need to go around the frame a couple times to cover all white areas.

4. Glue the frame (on three sides only!) onto the second rectangle. Leave one side open to stick the picture in. Let it dry.

5. As your picture frame is drying, create a small stand so your frame can sit on a table. Simply take a piece of foam-core board, about 2 inches by 3½ inches, and on the 2-inch side, bend back ½ inch. Then glue that ½ inch to the frame, making sure that the stand will sit on a flat surface.

6. At this time, if you want to add any rhinestones, pearls, buttons, plastic spiders, or anything else to the border of the frame, add them now using fabric glue. Let it dry.

7. Finally, put the picture of you and your friend in the frame, and you now have a gift that is sure to warm hearts for years to come!

Homemade Potpourri

It makes good "scents" to give this long-lasting gift to a friend.

What You'll Need

- dried rosebuds, leaves, and colored flowers
- string
- hangers
- nylons (any color)
- scissors
- newspapers
- box of whole cloves
- ribbon

Directions

1. Pick your flowers and leaves, allowing about an inch of stem on each. With string, tie several flowers and leaves together at the stems. Continue picking plants until you have several small bunches. Hang all the bunches upside down in a dark closet to dry for two weeks. You can tie the bunches to hangers with extra string if you like.

2. In the meantime, find some old nylons you don't mind destroying. You'll want to cut one nylon square for each potpourri bag. The squares can be 4, 6, or even 8 or 10 inches on a side.

3. After two weeks, lay out some newspapers and remove the flowers and leaves. Crumble the dried plants into small pieces on the nylon squares. For each potpourri bag, add about 12 whole cloves to the dried plants, then mix it well with your fingers.

4. Bring the corners of the nylon square together to create the potpourri bag. Secure it with a ribbon by tying it first into a tight knot around the nylon, then making a pretty bow.

One Step Further

If you're pressed for time, you can buy already-dried flowers from a craft store. For a different scent, substitute your favorite perfume for the whole cloves by spritzing a generous amount onto the plants before you place the mixture in the nylon.

Best Buddy Ball

ADULT SUPERVISION RECOMMENDED

Toss this personalized ball to your best pal to send her an extra-special message!

What You'll Need

- tracing paper (or other thin paper)
- pencil
- construction paper, various colors
- markers
- scissors
- glue

Directions

1. Trace the circle shown here onto your tracing paper, then cut it out. This is your circle pattern.

2. Using the pattern, outline twenty circles on the construction paper. You can use all one color, two colors, or as many different colors as you want. Then begin folding each circle along the three dotted lines shown in the illustration.

3. Now think about your friend. On each circle, write one word that describes her, such as "understanding," "honest," "funny," and "smart."

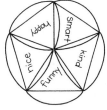

4. Begin gluing the folds of the circles together. Glue the first five circles together, joining the sides so that the five triangles point toward the center. Do the same with five other circles. You now have your top and bottom portions. Take the remaining ten circles, and glue a row around the base of the top portion. This will create a middle section to which you'll glue the base in step 6.

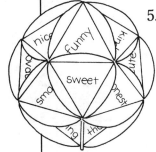

5. Now write an extra-special secret note to your friend. Be sure to put your name and the date on it. Then stick it inside your half-ball.

6. Finally, glue the bottom portion onto the rest of the ball. And there you have it—a unique buddy ball with a message inside!

Tic-Tac-Toe Bracelet

ADULT SUPERVISION RECOMMENDED

You'll delight the receiver of this fabulous gift, which is full of fashion and function! It's a hip bracelet that's meant to be worn anytime, but it's especially handy if you're looking for ways to pass the time. Here are the rules of the game. . . .

What You'll Need

- three felt squares, different colors
- bright yarn, 8 inches long
- Velcro strip, 5 inches long (found at any craft or sewing store)
- dice (optional)
- scissors
- rubber cement

Directions

1. First, you need to make your bracelet. Cut a bracelet out of one piece of felt that is at least 2¼ inches wide and long enough to fit around your wrist, with an inch or so left over. Cut four 2-inch pieces of yarn, then lay them out on the center of your bracelet in a tic-tac-toe board pattern. Each square should be approximately ¾ inch wide. Glue the yarn pieces down.

2. Cut nine ½-inch squares of Velcro. (You'll actually have 18 squares in total, since Velcro is one piece made up of two sheets that are locked together.) Be sure that all nine squares are the same size. You can use dice to trace the shape if you don't want to draw freehand. Set the Velcro pieces aside.

3. Next cut four ½-inch squares in one of the remaining colors of felt, making sure they're the same size as the Velcro pieces. Then cut five ½-inch squares from the other remaining color of felt.

4. Now, using the rubber cement, glue the back of the rough, sharp side of each Velcro square to each felt square. Glue the backs of the corresponding Velcro squares (the softer squares) inside the tic-tac-toe board.

RUBBER CEMENT

1st Color Felt

2nd Color Felt

Velcro

5. You should have a ½-inch strip of the two-sided Velcro remaining. Glue one side of the Velcro to one end of your bracelet and the second side to the other end. This will act as the fastener for the bracelet. Now you're ready to play!

How to Play

1. Find a friend to play with you. Then remove the nine felt squares from the bracelet.

2. Divide up the pieces of felt according to color (whoever goes first gets the shade with five pieces). Take turns placing squares onto the Velcro, with the aim of getting three squares in a row in any direction.

3. When you're done playing, return the nine pieces of felt to the bracelet for an armful of fashion and fun! (This bracelet comes in handy when you're waiting in line for lunch, or you need to pass a few minutes in class.)

Circle of Friendship
Wall Hanger

ADULT SUPERVISION RECOMMENDED

Your best friend will be "sew" delighted to hang up this handmade embroidered gift.

What You'll Need

- square of muslin material, 10 by 10 inches
- 8-inch embroidery hoop
- pencil
- needle
- embroidery thread
- scissors
- fabric glue
- strip of lace to fit around the 8-inch hoop

Directions

1. Place the muslin inside the embroidery hoop and tighten the screws so the fabric is taut across the top. Using your pencil, faintly write a message onto the fabric in block letters. (For example: BEST FRIENDS FOREVER! or YOU'RE AWESOME!)

2. Thread the needle and tie a knot at the end of the thread. Starting at the top of the first letter, come up through the bottom of the fabric with the needle. Pull tight. Wrap the thread around the needle three times as shown, and pull the needle back through the thread in the center. This is called a French knot.

3. Continue making these knots to cover all of the letters in your message. Make sure you place the knots right next to each other, without leaving spaces in between.

4. When your message is complete, position the fabric into the hoop again so that it's as tight as possible, and carefully trim away the excess fabric around the edges of the hoop. Now glue the strip of lace around the hoop to cover and decorate it. Your original artwork can be hung on the wall by placing the hoop over a nail.

46 Quickie Friendship Bracelet

This version of the traditional friendship bracelet will be a hands-down winner!

What You'll Need

- nine pieces of embroidery thread in three different shades, each about 9 to 10 inches long
- a knotting surface, like a book or table
- masking tape

Directions

1. First, group the nine pieces of embroidery thread together. Tie an overhand knot (illustrated here) about 2 inches from the end of the strands and tape the strands down on a book or table.

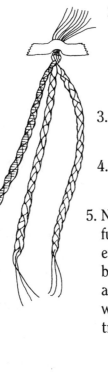

2. Take the first three pieces of the same color thread, and braid down to the bottom leaving a 1-inch tail. Repeat the process with the other two sets of embroidery thread. When you're finished with this step, you'll have three braids.

3. Now, braid all three pieces into one big braid, leaving a 1-inch tail at the bottom.

4. Tie the strand with an overhand knot to keep it secure.

5. Now comes the fun part! Tie the ends of the bracelet together around your friend's wrist. May she be forever reminded of your true-blue kinship!

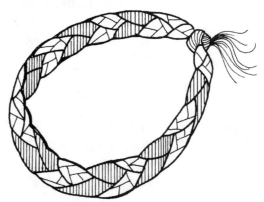

Flashy Look-Alike Fashions

Now it's a snap to double or triple up on fun fashions! Make outrageous look-alike ensembles that'll turn heads everywhere you go! This is a great project to do with a couple of friends.

What You'll Need

- newspapers
- wax paper
- dozens of fake gems and pearls, rhinestones and colored buttons
- pair of jeans and plain T-shirt for each friend
- fabric glue
- small, thin paintbrush for each friend

Directions

1. Lay out the newspapers on a clean surface to catch any glue drips, then set the T-shirts out flat. Place a couple layers of wax paper inside the shirt to prevent glue from seeping through. Choose which decorations you want to use on the T-shirt and begin putting them on the shirt. Do not do any gluing until you are finished designing. Try rhinestones around the neckline and sleeves, or a heart of pearls on the front. Anything goes, girl!

2. To fasten your creations, dip the paintbrush in the glue and apply it to the back of the decoration. Then, press it firmly onto the T-shirt and hold for a few seconds. Continue gluing until all the decorations have been placed. Set the T-shirt aside.

3. Repeat the same procedure on the jeans. (You don't need to put wax paper in the jeans—the jean material is heavy enough to keep glue from seeping through.) Try putting your initials on the back pocket with miniature buttons or running a row of rhinestones down the outside of each leg.

4. Let your wild wardrobe dry overnight. When it's time to launder these creation sensations, wash only by hand.

One Step Further

With any beads, jewels, or buttons you have left over, glue them onto a plain headband or a pair of barrettes.

Charming Choker

ADULT SUPERVISION RECOMMENDED

Your friend will get "all choked up" when she receives this pretty present.

What You'll Need

- strip of white lace, 1 foot long and ½ inch wide
- strip of dark green, red, or black velvet ribbon, 1 foot long and 1 inch wide
- scissors
- fabric glue
- 1-inch square of Velcro
- a small cameo brooch (found at craft stores)

Directions

1. Measure the piece of velvet to fit around your neck, then add ¾ inch to each end and cut. Measure the lace the same way and cut.

2. Apply fabric glue to the back of the lace, then place it in the center of the velvet ribbon so that the velvet shows at the top and bottom of the choker and the lace runs around the middle.

3. Glue a square of Velcro to each end of the choker so that it will fasten securely around your neck.

4. Now glue the cameo brooch in the center of the choker on top of the lace. Let it dry for several hours. You're ready to present this charming, yet easy-to-make gift!

 # Natural Color Bead Bracelet

ADULT SUPERVISION RECOMMENDED
Create ultra-cool designs from soft bread dough, and when the dough dries, put together a masterpiece bracelet that will go down in history.

What You'll Need

- three slices of white bread, crusts removed
- 3 teaspoons white glue
- ⅛ teaspoon liquid detergent
- mixing bowl
- spoon
- old earrings and brooches to indent into the beads
- toothpicks
- spool wire
- bracelet clasp (found at craft stores)
- scissors
- varnish

Directions

1. To make the dough for the beads, crumble the bread into a bowl, then add the glue and liquid detergent. Stir the mixture with a spoon for a few seconds, then knead it with your hands. The dough will be sticky at first. When it starts to form into a ball and is no longer sticky, the dough is ready to use. Hint: If it seems too sticky even after kneading, add more crumbled bread.

2. Make little balls (about twelve balls, each ¼ inch thick) from the dough with your hands. Press down on six of the balls with your palm to make round, flatter beads. Leave them thick enough so that you can pierce through the side with a toothpick. The remaining six balls are for round beads on your bracelet.

3. Use the old jewelry with intricately carved surfaces to press into the beads to make beautiful indentations. Also, use your imagination to create your own patterns and designs.

4. Arrange the flat and round beads in the order you want them on the bracelet. On one of the flat beads, use a toothpick to carve the date and your initials in the dough.

66

5. Pierce holes through the side of each bead as shown. That way, the flat beads will lie flat against the wrist when strung.

6. Measure the spool wire around your wrist to see how much wire you'll need. Then, add another 2 inches on each end and cut the wire. Starting 2 inches from the end, string the beads on the spool wire. Then take your bracelet clasp and tie each of the two parts onto the two ends of the bracelet. Be sure to double-check the length of the bracelet first for a perfect fit!

7. Let the dough dry for twelve hours, then spray with varnish or lacquer for a shiny, natural look.

Year of Fun

This special gift will give your friend a whole year of fun things to do, along with happy thoughts of you.

What You'll Need

- scratch paper
- felt tip pens, various colors
- any calendar, any size
- variety of stickers

Directions

1. On scratch paper, write down activities that you and your friend enjoy doing together, as well as several activities that your friend would enjoy doing by herself. Some ideas might be: taking a bubble bath, going for a walk, playing with a pet, baking cookies, starting a journal, and boy-watching!

2. Then grab your pens and begin writing in the calendar the special activities for your friend to do throughout the year. Don't forget to include extra-fun things to do over the holidays. For instance, on July 4, you may write, "Spend the day with Lori at the park, then watch the fireworks with our favorite guys!" Write down both activities for the two of you to do together, as well as activities that she can do on her own.

3. You don't need to fill every single day, but if a week or a month is looking empty, fill it up with cute, cheery stickers or little pictures that you draw yourself.

4. Don't forget that every day you put down an activity for the two of you to do together, you need to write it down in your own calendar. Your friend will thank you for giving her such a great year to look forward to!

One Step Further

This can be done on a scaled-down version. You can give your friend a special month of fun activities, with something different to do every day of the month.

Activities for Two

"The most I can do for my friend is simply to be his friend."
—Henry David Thoreau

Whether you're spending time together on a rainy day or taking an afternoon study break, here are some terrific things you and your best friend can do together. The Study Buddy Book Holder (page 12) is fun to make and will inspire both of you to finish that weekend homework! You can write cute and encouraging messages to each other and attach them to the book holders. You might even surprise your friend by slipping a Nature's Own Bookmark (page 29) in one of her books when she's not looking!

For some really creative fun, make Terrific Tees for Two (page 16). These colorful shirts will tell everyone you're totally in sync with each other. And if you really want to get dressed up, you can make matching Hassle-Free Headbands for Two (page 34), Lace Barrettes (page 50), Charming Chokers (page 65), and Buddy-Up Buttons (page 55). Then have a funky fashion show starring the two of you!

For a special keepsake you'll want to hold on to forever, do a Makin' Memories Diary (page 26). You and your best friend will have fun designing it together. When you're done, write about the memories you've shared throughout your friendship and include your favorite sayings, places to go, songs, and anything else you can think of. Then take turns writing in it. You can pass it back and forth from week to week or month to month, writing notes to each other. There is no limit to the things you can do with this personal treasure!

Special Gifts for Your Friends

"You give but little when you give of your possessions.
It is when you give of yourself that you truly give."

—Kahlil Gibran

Has one of your best friends experienced any of the following recently?

♥ The guy she likes has his eyes on someone else.
♥ She studied hard for a test, yet she scored poorly.
♥ Her parents are getting a divorce.
♥ Her favorite pet ran away.
♥ Her soccer team lost the championship.

Whether your friend has had any one of these things happen to her, or she's just had a string of bad days, give her a little gift to lift her spirits—made with love by you!

How about making something to show her what a terrific person you think she is? With the Best Buddy Ball (page 59) you can let her know all the things you really like and admire about her.

To show her how proud you are of her many accomplishments, you can make a Baby, It's You! wall decoration for her room (page 23). She will be honored! You can also create this wall craft with a humorous theme. Decorate the board with funny pictures of your friends, favorite comic strip characters, hilarious jokes, and whatever else you can think of that will bring a smile to your friend's face.

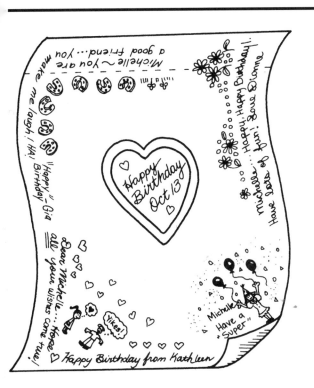

When her birthday rolls around, surprise your pal by gathering all of her friends together to make a Best Buddies' Bed Sheet (page 18). You'll have fun making it, and she'll enjoy reading what you've written. This gift will remind her always of how special she is to you and her other friends.

Just for Fun

Even gift wrapping can be personalized, so check out It's a Wrap! (page 17) and the Folded Paper Gift Box (page 52). The time and effort spent on these ideas will touch your friend as much as any gift you could give her!

Let's Party!

(A Guide to Hosting Your Own Craft Party)

"A friend is a person with whom you dare to be yourself."

—Anonymous

Show your friends how much you care about them by hosting a friendship craft party! It's a cool way to spend time together, and what better reason is there to have a party? You'll have tons of fun making crafts, and everyone will have something special to take home with them. Your friends will love the idea!

Cool Invitations

Before writing out the invitations, make sure you get parental approval on the number of guests you can invite. Write out your guest list, and double-check it to be certain you haven't forgotten anyone.

You can buy invitations from a card or gift store, or you can make your own. If you decide to design your own invitations, decorate them to match your theme, either by the crafts you are making or by the colors you are using. Be sure to include all the important information about your party, such as:

♥ Who's hosting the party
♥ What the occasion is
♥ Where it's being held (and directions if needed)
♥ When it is
♥ Any special instructions, such as things to bring, what to wear, and so on

Also ask your friends to R.S.V.P. as soon as possible and include your phone number. Let them know you'll be making crafts, so that they can wear or bring old clothing.

If you have the time, make your invitations extra-special by including a special craft item in the envelope with each invitation. Here are some ideas to get your creative juices flowing. You can choose the one that's perfect for you and your pals!

♥ For a little suspense, give each person you invite a Secret Code Bracelet (page 54) with a message on it and tell her you will reveal the hidden meaning at your party. (For instance, WHSCFTW stands for We'll Have Super-Cool Fun This Weekend.)

♥ Include a Quick 'n' Easy Ring (page 25) with each invitation. This simple yet colorful item will remind your friends that your party is coming up.

♥ Make each person a personalized Heart-to-Heart Pin (page 32) and ask her to wear it to the party. This craft is especially helpful if you are introducing new friends at your party—no need for name tags with these cool pins!

Creating the Scene

As you prepare for your party, you can cover the walls with decorations or keep the setting simple with a few strategically placed festive items. A single large craft can really jazz up the whole room! For instance, the Hanging Friendship Tree (page 8) is the perfect party piece to show off your friendships using the mementos and pictures you've collected over the years. You can even include items from the interests you

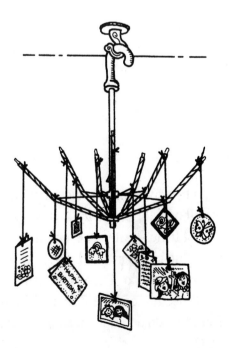

and your buddies share (such as a picture of your favorite music group or a mini soccer ball). Your friends will be delighted when they see this creative collection. When the party's over, you can hang the craft in your room.

The Lantern of Friendship on page 41 makes a pretty table centerpiece and adds a charming touch when placed in your entryway or on your porch. Your friends will be "enlightened" by your creativity!

Another great decoration is the Circle of Friendship Wall Hanger on page 62. You can embroider sentimental sayings or a special welcome to your guests. This is also a terrific keepsake.

For some colorful but simple decorations, try making a few bouquets of Forever Friendship Flowers (page 38) to brighten up the room. Put some in the bathroom, on the kitchen table, or wherever else you will be spending time.

Details, Details, Details!

No party would be complete without some special treats. Ask for a parent's help in preparing a few favorite foods to snack on during the party. And of course you'll want to play all those songs your friends love to sing along with while you are making crafts. This will really get things shaking!

Perfect Party Crafts

The purpose of the party is to have fun and celebrate your friendship, so try to relax and enjoy yourself. This will be a lot easier to do if you set up the materials you will need for your crafts ahead of time. That way everyone can concentrate on the task at hand. You can select any of the crafts in this book to work on, but decide before the party which ones you would like to do. Then make sure you have enough time and all of the materials you will need to complete them. The party can be just as fun if you focus on one super craft or do a couple of smaller ones.

One idea perfect for parties is to make a friendship time capsule with the Keepsake Box on page 44. Ask your friends to bring pictures and special mementos of the times you've shared. Be sure to tell them the items are for a time capsule and won't be returned for a long, long time!

Decorate the box together, then fill it with the objects brought by everyone. Have each person write a letter to herself about what she thinks she'll be doing in the future. Drop the letters into the box, then seal it with heavy tape. Put the box in a safe place and promise to leave it untouched for the next 10 years. Make a pact with your friends to have a reunion and reveal the contents of your time capsule at that time.

Helpful Hints

To make the preparation easier, why not have your guests help out? Ask each friend to bring a different material for a craft that you will be making. Or if you are making individual crafts, such as the Flashy Look-Alike Fashions, ask each guest to bring her own item (in this case, a T-shirt). Take a close look at the list of crafts you want to do and figure out what items would be best to have your guests bring. Be specific on the invitations about what they will need and how much to buy.

- For a really charming keepsake, you can make bracelets, such as the Official Initial Charm Bracelet on page 36. Each person will receive her own charm bracelet to remind her of all her creative friends! She will think about friendship each time she wears it.

- Make a Chain of Friendship (page 46). With this craft each guest can write a personal note to her friends *and* have one to read from each of them when she's at home.

♡ The "Friends Only!" Doorknob Hanger (page 19) is a neat craft each girl can use for her bedroom. Or make an African Love Bead Necklace (page 14) that you can wear to school. Both of these projects let each person express herself as an individual while bonding with the group.

♡ If your party is a sleep-over, try this dreamy craft, Sew 'n' Sleep Autographs (page 20). You can swap stories and share secrets while everyone signs the pillow and draws little pictures. Then give the pillow to the guest of honor or the hostess as a souvenir of the evening.

♡ A nice way to capture memories from the party is to take pictures. Ask a parent to take pictures of the whole group in wacky poses, then make Do-It-Yourself Personalized Frames (page 56). As fun party favors, give each person one of the pictures for her frame to remember the evening long after the party's over.

These are just a few ideas to get you and your friends in that creative mindset. The following pages will help you with every detail of your party planning. You may want to copy these pages into a notebook or photcopy them for each party you have!

The 4-Week Party Countdown

4 WEEKS

___ Choose a theme and focus on particular crafts that would be fun to make.

___ Pick the date and time for your party.

___ Check with your parents on the date of your party and the theme.

3 WEEKS

___ Fill out the Party Specifics list and the Guest List from page 79. Have your parents check over them to make sure they are okay.

___ Fill out the Crafts list from page 80. Decide what you would like your friends to bring and who will bring specific items.

___ Buy or make your invitations. Also make any small crafts you would like to include with your invitations.

2 WEEKS

___ Deliver your invitations.

___ Complete the Decorations, Music, and Food lists on pages 79 and 80. Mark the items that you will need to buy at the store.

1 WEEK

___ Call the friends who have not R.S.V.P.'d. (If someone cannot come, you will need to buy the materials you assigned her to bring.)

___ Go shopping for the materials and other items you will need.

___ Start putting together your decorations.

THE DAY BEFORE

___ Read through the instructions of the crafts you plan to make. Double-check that you have everything you will need.

___ Call to remind your friends to bring the items for the crafts.

___ Collect old newspapers and clothing to use when making your crafts.

___ Set out the decorations and materials you will be using at your party.

___ Prepare any food that will keep overnight.

THE DAY!

___ Prepare the rest of the food and drinks.

___ Get your music set up.

___ Have fun!

AFTER THE PARTY

___ Put away leftover food and drinks.

___ Pick up all the trash.

___ Take down the decorations (move them to your room if you would like to keep them).

___ Store the extra materials to use for your next craft project.

___ Vacuum and finish cleaning up the room.

Step-by-Step to Do List

Party Specifics

Theme: _____

Date: _____

Time: _____

Place: _____

Guest List

People to invite	Invitation sent	R.S.V.P.
_____	_____	_____
_____	_____	_____
_____	_____	_____
_____	_____	_____
_____	_____	_____

Decorations

Need to make	Need to buy
_____	_____
_____	_____
_____	_____

Food

Need to make	Need to buy
_____	_____
_____	_____
_____	_____

Music

Songs/Groups to play

Who will bring it?

_____   _____

_____   _____

_____   _____

Crafts

Craft: _____

Materials needed

Who will bring it?

_____   _____

_____   _____

_____   _____

_____   _____

_____   _____

_____   _____

Craft: _____

Materials needed

Who will bring it?

_____   _____

_____   _____

_____   _____

_____   _____

_____   _____

_____   _____